Y2K

How to Protect Your Family In

THE QUIET
CRISIS

Y2K
How to Protect Your Family In
THE QUIET CRISIS

Todd Phillips
Darren McMaster

Published by Safe 2000, Inc.
San Antonio, TX

Cover Design by Darren McMaster

Photo of Darren McMaster by Rick Shelley, Photographer
Photo of Todd Phillips by Paul Carr

ISBN # 0-9667797-0-3

DEDICATION

To God, Kelly, Julie and Gaby
for their faith and encouragement in this project
and its potential to impact the lives of those who read it.

Thank you all.

We love you.

AKNOWLEDGEMENT

Our most sincere appreciation goes out to Sarah Snelling and Carol Graves for their tenacity, foresight and direction in editing this book.

• Contents •

• Foreword •

1999 will be the single most important year in the history of mankind. Life as we know it could irrevocably change with the simple changing of a date.

On January 1, 2000, we will step into the Third Millennium. We pray it will be a millennium full of peace and prosperity.

Yet the minute we enter into the Third Millennium many of our computers will re-enter the Second Millennium. At 12:01, on the morning of January 1, 2000, the Millennium Bug (also known as the Year 2000 Problem or Y2K) will be born. This computer programming glitch, if uncorrected, could cause millions of computers to malfunction. For the first time in human history a technological error could disrupt the entire industrialized world in one day. This malfunction and its consequences are the focuses of this book.

For the next year you will see, hear, and read numerous versions of what could possibly happen. In this book, we will attempt to maintain the middle ground of the issue and cover both sides of the story. Some say that nothing is going to happen while others say the world is coming to an end. We know that somewhere in between these extremes lies the answer. We feel it is critical that you read about and understand the potential impact of this crisis. We encourage you, at the conclusion of this book, to continue researching the problems and solutions. In the end, you must come up with your own conclusions based on the information you have gathered and plan an appropriate path for you and your family.

At Safe 2000 our objective is not to cause fear or start a panic. We believe that both are unnecessary and unwarranted. Our goal is to inform and educate the general public about the realities of the Y2K problem. We will attempt to provide a clear and rational discussion, in a short and concise manner, on most of the major points

of the problem. Specifically, we will define how this problem could affect the lives of average individuals and what they can do to protect themselves. Yet, our primary objective is to create awareness to the problem and encourage action on both the individual and corporate level.

The following scenarios may seem extreme to some, and granted, some of them are. We did this in an attempt to simply drive home the seriousness of the problem. The biggest problem we face today is corporate complacency. Failing to take the problem seriously and failing to properly complete the steps to solve the problem could severely slow our growth into the new millennium.

• Chapter 1 •

The Problem

"No the sky is not falling, it's just that your computers won't work! ...Telling the public that the computers can't do arithmetic, and they face imminent danger, is such an abstract concept that most do not take it seriously."
Testimony of Alan Simpson before the US House of Representatives. June 22nd, 1998 [1]

"85% of current mainframe systems will be in production at the end of the century and less than 50% will be year 2000 compliant..."
Gartner Group [2]

What Is It?

Fair warning! After the Year 2000 computer problem is described to you it may seem like nothing more than a simple programming issue that the technical nerds at the office or at your local computer store can solve in no time. It may be nearly inconceivable for your mind to accept that this deceptively tiny computer 'glitch' can possibly affect you and your family, let alone your travel plans and investments . . . BUT IT CAN!

The problem has its roots in the dawning age of computers. When computer programs were first developed, programmers decided to use a two-digit system to represent the year. Instead of a four-digit number, for example, 1998 would be represented as '98,' 1999 would be represented as '99' and so on. The problem arises when computer dating reaches the year 2000 - the computer will then show '00' for the year. Computers will mistakenly perceive '00' as the year 1900 causing computer failures as we near January 1, 2000.

Why did the programmers choose to do this? Some suggest that they simply didn't expect the system to last this long. Others suggest that the programmers wanted to save memory, which, at the time, was quite expensive. Finally, they could have simply not been thinking! At any rate, the problem is real and there is a deadline

As you can see this sounds minor, if not irrelevant at first. It did to us. The problem, however, has precedent. The IBM 360, one of International Business Machine's (IBM) first computers, could not read or process dates past December 31, 1969. These computers began to fail at midnight on the 31st. IBM, realizing the global significance of the matter, found a temporary solution by telling 360 computer users to lie to their computer about the date. Then, IBM eventually created a longer-term solution to the problem.[3]

This issue is not one, which merely hinges on theory. It is not a question of 'if' it will happen or 'when' it will happen, but how serious the consequences will be - that is the $64,000 question (or $64M or $64B).

Where Are We Today?

First of all, we don't have to wait until the year 2000 to see if problems will arise because they already have. Department stores, high schools and colleges, and state Motor Vehicle

Departments are finding that referencing dates after January 1, 2000, result in some rather bizarre issues. One department store found that their computers shut down after a credit card with the expiration date of '00' was swiped through a machine. High schools and colleges are showing students as graduating 99 years ago and driver's licenses are coming up as already expired if their expiration date is after January 1, 2000. [4] These are just a few examples.

How close are we to solving the problem? Not very close. Peter de Jager is a consultant who has attempted to raise public awareness about the seriousness of the year 2000 bug. He stated several alarming realities regarding the problem in his testimony before Congress on May 14, 1996:

1. The deadline is real, immovable and cannot be missed.
2. We have less than 140 weekends left to complete the task.
3. Less than 35% of North American businesses have begun.
4. Those active have found this to be the most complex project they've ever attempted.
5. There are unique, non-technical obstacles in our path.
6. The I.S. community suffers under a delusion of infallible confidence, despite a proven track record of no greater than 14%.
7. The sense of urgency required to complete this task on time is absent.[5]

In other words, nobody was taking it seriously in 1996. Even today, few are taking it as seriously or with as much attention as is needed to even hope to have a solution to the problem within the allotted time.

The statistics have improved since 1996, but they still fall far short of where we should be in attacking the problem. They show that, although the community at large is now aware of the problem, few have done anything to address it. In the Fall of 1997, a survey was done on two thousand Canadian businesses in reference to their efforts, if any, to address the year 2000 computer problem. Statistics Canada did the survey. The results were as follows:

1. "Although more than 90% of businesses are aware of Y2K, only about 50% appear to have taken actions to address the challenge. Only one firm in ten had a formal action plan.
2. Only 13% of the executives aware of Y2K had asked their business partners about their state of readiness.
3. In the key transportation, communication and utilities sector, half of the large firms surveyed had not takes formal action to address Y2K. "Yet these firms are often mission critical to the national or local economy."
4. Only a third of the primary industries sector had taken any action. This suggests that the whole supply chain is at risk."[6]

Are you still wondering how this all affects you personally? Read on.

The Problem Is Global

The problem is global in scope but, its effects will be experienced in large part by the individual. For this reason, it is necessary to explain the breadth of the problem before attempting to address the potential impact to the individual.

Many of our trading partners around the globe are said to be six to eighteen months behind the United States in their efforts to deal with this problem in their own country.[7] In a sworn testimony given to the Subcommittee on Technology, Committee on Science of the U.S. House of Representatives, some alarming facts were given in regard to this issue in other countries:

1.   "Japan, our number two trading partner, is already in the midst of a recession. Their banks have been fighting to maintain solvency. Surely more will fall as a result of the breakdown in the Asian marketplace. Morris Goldstein of the Institute for International Economics here in Washington said that, "[Japan] was set for a truly world-class banking crisis." Our financial community here in the U.S. is becoming increasingly concerned by the lack of assurances they

are getting from Japanese banks that they will be ready in time."

2. "The Mexican government, our third largest trading partner, appointed a year 2000 task force just two weeks ago, "to look into the problem." They had their first meeting on October 30th. The private sector there has just begun to talk seriously about the problem."

3. "A recent survey conducted in the UK and sponsored by Cap Gemini indicated that ten percent (10%) of businesses would fail to meet the Y2K deadline. As some in this group are very large businesses, nearly thirty percent (30%) of the country's GDP would be threatened. Small and medium size enterprises are of particular concern as they remain complacent, in spite of the fact that demand will exceed supply for skilled labor by April of 1998, according to a story which appeared in PA news."

4. "Germany, France, and Italy are trailing the U.S. significantly in their efforts to address the issue. In fact, the entire European community is behind in their work as most of their time and resources have been focused on the significant challenge of converting to a single currency by the turn of the century."

5. "In Australia, the RBA (similar to our Federal Reserve Bank) has said, "many banks do not seem to have a good feel for the size of their [foreign exchange] settlement risk." The RBA expressed concern that so much of the work remains uncompleted."[8]

It is extremely important for each of us to understand this problem, but it still may not be hitting home. The best way to explain the ramifications of the Y2K problem is to create a scenario.

Suppose you have a checking account with a bank that is Y2K compliant, meaning they have successfully corrected the problem throughout their internal network of computers. No problem, then. Right? Wrong! Say you receive a check from someone whose bank is non-compliant, and, as a result, the check you received from her does not get cleared. The money does not go into your account and you write checks against funds that do not exist.

Let's take the problem to a different level.

Suppose you have several Certificates of Deposit in the bank that are set to mature after the January 1, 2000 date. You are relying on that interest income each year for retirement income (to pay mortgage, utilities, food, etc.). Your bank is not Y2K compliant and incorrectly identifies the maturity date of your C.D. as '00' or the year 1900 and your interest check is delayed indefinitely while the problem is fixed. You should be able to just go to the bank and straighten things out. Right? Not, if the other thousands of C.D. owners beat you to the bank. The problem could take weeks or months to fix, and meanwhile, your bills continue to stack up.

Your bank is linked via computer to every other bank in the world. Your bank may have solved the Y2K problem but the banks it deals with daily around the world may not be. In that case everything from your checking accounts to your investments to your auto and home loans could be adversely affected.

The problem is not limited to the institutions you deal with directly. You are indirectly connected to every institution that your institution is connected to and so on and so on. The problem is of global proportions, yet its effect could be felt most by the individual.

• Chapter 2 •

Solving the Y2K Problem

"...Today we have hundreds of millions of computers and devices and tens of billions of embedded chips - many of which will not accurately read the year 2000. When you have that many of them, if only a small percentage of them don't accurately read the date, then the world has a problem. And unless the old lines of code are fixed, the problems, of course, will be serious."
Vice President Al Gore, July 14, 1998 [1]

"There is no way we're going to fix 100% of all the computer systems around the world in time"
Edward Yardeni, Chief Economist with
Deutsche Morgan Grenfell [2]

Lack of Programmers

Fixing the Y2K problem is not a significant technical challenge. In fact, like the description of the problem itself, the solution is disarming in its perceived simplicity. There are a number of serious side issues that companies must address that we will not go into here because their relevance is secondary to the issue of time. That's right, time is the enemy in our collective efforts to avoid the repercussions of the coming crisis. We simply do not have the time to correct the millions of lines of programming in the 250 million or more PCs in the world. There are not enough people who know what they are doing to manage all the corrections that must be done between now and December 31, 1999.

Programming Pitfalls

The general consensus in months past was that this was an issue limited mainly to large mainframe computers. This misperception is obviously not the case. The problem seems to become even more logistically impossible when you consider all of the uses for the computer chip. They are used in building security systems, elevators, automobiles, microwaves, VCRs, copy machines, some mobile phones, satellites, and on and on and on. The list is, for the purposes of this book, endless. We are inescapably tied to computer chips and, unfortunately then, we are also unable to escape the potential flood of issues resulting from the year 2000 computer problem.

We can also look at it from another angle. Cheerleaders are known for making human pyramids. More often than not, they put people at the base who are the strongest in the group, then they build on that base until the pyramid is complete. Barring some unforeseen variable, a pyramid built by this process will be strong and not fall. However, if one of the cheerleaders at the base of the pyramid is injured in some way, enough to cause them to become so weak as not to support the pyramid, the entire structure is in trouble. To make matters worse, in this scenario, the individual who has been injured is unaware of the seriousness of the injury and proceeds to get into position. The pyramid then builds on that base and is completed, only to fall in on itself because of the silent injury that was supposedly minor and insignificant to the overall strength of the pyramid.

The same thing has, in effect, happened with the Y2K problem. Over time, the foundation of our entire society has become computers. They are the strong and dependable workhorses supporting our entire government and economy. We have built upon that foundation a pyramid that towers above the base creating a magnificent structure which combines finance, government and homes that are almost completely reliant on high technology. The only problem is that when the foundation was created, it was created with a weakness of which we were all unaware. A seemingly insignificant weakness could ultimately topple the mighty pyramid of our society.

Another part of this scenario that merits some discussion is the placement of this injured person. When the individual is first chosen for the base of the pyramid, there are only six people making up the structure. Over time, however, the pyramid becomes a huge structure with over 500 people, one on top of the other, making the structure significantly larger than was ever imagined. So, when the injured person is placed at the base, the structure being supported is far greater than the base was ever expected to support. The destruction, then, parallels the size of the structure built.

This part of the scenario should help you to understand how this small problem can potentially create such chaos. The structure we have built (upon this base of technology) is thousands of times more immense and far reaching than the creators of the first computers could have ever dreamed. Consequently, they did the best they could with the information available at the time.

Finally, there is one additional comment regarding the placement of this injured person. If this person were placed at or near the top of the pyramid, the injury being the same, the destruction, if any, to the overall pyramid would be minor. Yet, the deeper this individual is placed, the greater the potential damage. The worst place for this person to be, then, is at the foundation where the entire structure is forced to rely on this injured person for its overall integrity.

This example illustrates the case with Y2K. Computers are the bedrock of our society with regard to nearly everything including communication, transportation, finance and government. Is this information hitting home?

Apathy

Surprisingly, there has also been an overwhelming apathy on the part of the business community. There was this idea floating around that if the problem really did exist then the ever popular 'someone' would write a program to fix the problem.

It never has been that simple! There is no broad-stroking formula to solve the problem at hand.

Now, many companies are realizing that the solution is much more involved than they had previously thought. In fact, the average large company may spend $40 million to fix the problem.[3] The cost lies in the arduous process of literally going through line by line of data, looking for the mistake, and then correcting it each time it shows up. The estimated cost for reviewing code is about one dollar a line. Some companies have estimated that they have over 200 million lines of data to review. This puts the latest estimates for the total cost of solving the Y2K issue globally at between 300 and 600 BILLION DOLLARS.[4]

Human Error

Another consideration in the mix is human error. Think about it. If a programmer is given the task to review 500,000 lines of computer code, what are the chances that he or she might miss one, or five, or one hundred lines of non-compliant code in 500,000? The chances are extremely high. If those lines of code that are missed are functionally linked to the rest of the program, then the problem still exists. So, if a program is reviewed, corrected to the best of the programmer's ability, and then run through a battery of tests - if it fails again - the programmer will be forced to go through the 500,000 lines over and over until it's done right. The most exhaustive part of the process is in the testing. There is no easy answer.

Large corporations as well as government agencies have thousands of different programs on their computers. Many of these programs are not documented sufficiently and the mere existence of some has been forgotten. Put simply, there are hundreds of programs that house deeply embedded code that haven't been touched in years. Making matters worse, the programmer who created the codes in the program, may have left the company without leaving any programming information with the next man.

Finally, many of the programming languages whose names are familiar to most of us, like COBOL, were programmed by people who developed their own individual code words to create their programs. Computer language is much like our verbal language in that there are many ways to say the same thing. Another problem arises as the programmers of today attempt to decode the program language of another person.[5]

We're On a Fixed Time-frame

Make no mistake; we are on a collision course with the Millennium. The date is fixed and the problem is real. We have less than 80 weeks to deal with the issue, but most companies and many individuals are ignoring what could alarmingly damaging to everyone. This problem is an unavoidable event that deserves the attention of everyone, including you.

All of this information should drive home the fact that the Y2K problem's scope is global and its effects could very well reach into your home, your time, and your wallet.

• Chapter 3 •

A Report on the Government

"The Year 2000 (Y2K) computer crisis is now upon us and the federal government is even more woefully unprepared than the rest of society. The implications are ominous. Medicare, the IRS, the Federal Aviation Administration and other basic agencies are operating on utterly out-of-date technology. It doesn't take much imagination to see how dreadfully wrong things could go."
Steve Forbes[1]

The US Government's Progress is Inadequate

Our government's response to the Y2K issue has been totally inadequate up to this point. Our government has the opportunity and responsibility to put forth an aggressive effort to not only make its citizens aware of the problem, but to work tirelessly to fix the problem as it relates to all government agencies.

Vice President Al Gore stated,

". . . [Y2K] is a challenge that exists on four different levels. First of all, it's a challenge to the Federal Government. With more than 7000 mission critical systems at the federal level, carrying out functions ranging from Social Security payments to air traffic control, it is critical that our electronic systems run effectively and efficiently."

"Secondly, it's a challenge to state and local governments. States use computers to run vital public health and safety systems, from Medicaid to unemployment insurance to water treatment plants."

"Third, it's a special challenge to the private sector. Virtually every American business, both large and small, has a stake in our information economy and ultimately has to take personal responsibility for fixing their own system . . ."

"Fourth, it is an international challenge. In a world with hundreds of different languages, the way in which our computers speak to one another across national boundaries drives our markets, our jobs, and our future."[2]

Vice President Gore masterfully summarizes each of his four points and adequately addresses the issue as it pertains to each point. However, he fails to address the fifth issue, just as nearly everyone else who speaks out on the Y2K problem. The fifth challenge is the individual challenge.

There is a frightening theme that has developed among those in power, both in the government and in the private sector. This theme permeates all levels of discussion regarding the year 2000 problem. It is this ever-present, categorical separation of the citizens of the United States from any discussion pertaining to this matter. What about the personal computers which sit on the desks of millions of homes across the land? What about the lack of effort by anyone to make the general public aware of this problem as it relates to not only the national economy, the national government, and international affairs, but also to the average citizen? This issue is where the high-tech comedy of errors could hit the hardest. If these questions are important to you, read on. They will be discussed in later chapters.

Departmental Progress in Government

IRS

The IRS, the agency that collects taxes and distributes tax refunds has been making efforts to solve the Y2K issue for some time. Yet, the Commissioner of the IRS told The Wall Street Journal in their April 22, 1998 issue that,

"There's no point in sugarcoating the problem. If we don't fix the century-date problem, we will have a situation scarier than the average disaster movie you might see on a Sunday night. Twenty-one months from now, there could be 90 million tax payers who don't get their refunds, and 95% of the revenue stream of the United States could be jeapordized."[3]

This statement isn't from some random dooms-dayer, but from the Commissioner of the Internal Revenue service.

Some employees at the IRS are not as extreme in their statements about how the Y2K issue might affect the agency. On April 1, 1998, Arthur Gross, the Chief Information Officer of the IRS left the agency. He left only three months after Charles O. Rossotti became the agency's new commissioner. It has been said that the two held differing views on how to go about modernizing the IRS. Mr. Gross was an avid supporter and very candid in his belief that the Y2K issue would require monumental effort on the part of the agency to become Y2K compliant by the turn of the century. His departure could be a setback in those efforts.

Mr. Rossotti was optimistic, however, in his address to the House Ways and Means Oversight Committee, where he suggested that the bulk of the work would be done before the start of the 1999 filing season. This comment is a promising one from someone who should be apprised of the progress within his agency. Yet, this dichotomy of opinions is common among top officials in many of the agencies, even from the same official who says one thing then another, leaving the public confused about the true progress.

These officials are most likely not trying to be ambiguous, or even to contradict themselves from interview to interview, nor are they, for the most part, attempting to hide the real issue. As they receive updates on progress within their agencies they become more aware of the scope of the problem and must update their prior statements to reflect new information. Sometimes the new information causes them to put a more positive slant on their reports, but more often, new information forces those in power to reassess the Y2K problem and respond more negatively and with more pessimism as the Millennium draws near.

A true sign the IRS could be in trouble would be increased talks about a nationwide flat tax. If in fact the lawmakers begin legislation toward a flat tax, this could be a direct result of the lack of readiness in the IRS.

FAA

Many who are relatively well informed on the issue are very concerned over the potential effect Y2K could have on the Federal Aviation Administration, specifically flights on and around January 1, 2000. The FAA is as aware of the problem, as the IRS is, and is working diligently to fix it. We must remember, though, that the interconnectivity of computers is of paramount importance. The problem will eventually be fixed. But, the problem may not be 100% fixed before the millennium. Again, if only 5% of the computers, for example, are not fixed at the FAA, those 5% could adversely affect the other 95% of compliant computers.

As with other areas of government and business, most people are focusing their attention on the global scope of the problem. Many are suggesting that a slowdown of global transportation for any length of time could be very depressing for global business activity.[4] Think about all of the businesses that rely on shipping freight via air transport. All of the overnight delivery services like Federal Express rely almost completely on air transportation to deliver packages with an overnight guarantee. Many companies rely on these services to effectively run their businesses.

The FAA released an updated version in April, 1997, of a "Guidance Document for the Year 2000 Date Conversion" which was originally issued several months before in September, 1996. Here are some excerpts from this document that are cause for concern relating to the result of the FAA's efforts to address Y2K:

"Much has been written about the problems facing business applications that compute such things as ages, expiration dates, and due dates, by subtracting one year from another. There is much less information available about the impact on more sophisticated systems, such as radar processors, communications processors, and satellite systems." [Emphasis added.]

"The systems affected are primarily legacy systems, although all systems should be checked to ensure they correctly handle a four-digit year field. The types of systems include mainframe, client/server, workstations, distributed systems, such as radar processors, and communication processors." [Emphasis added.]

"The FAA does not have direct control over updating of commercial application software, commercial off-the-shelf items, or non-developmental items on which many critical systems depend. Many FAA systems depend on data supplied by other systems running on different platforms. Many FAA systems receive data from and provide data to systems external to the FAA. In all these cases, dates need to be changed at the same time and in the same manner, or bridges need to be built to handle conversion of dates from one format to the other. In many cases the developers have long since retired or been promoted and the current owners do not know what all the components are or what interfaces are."

"The FAA has been downsizing and many of the senior information systems people who developed the software have retired. Even if funds are available to pay for contract programming support, this support is going to become increasingly difficult to find as the deadline approaches.

"There is concern that some of the products that the FAA is using will not be upgraded to be Year 2000 compliant. In recent years, a number of large companies have bought out their competitors and continued maintaining their competitor's products even though they perform the same function as their own products. It is not clear that these vendors are going to make all the products Year 2000 compliant. If they drop support on some products, anyone using the abandoned products will need to upgrade or convert to another product. There is also a concern that some vendors will simply go out of business rather than incur the cost of upgrading their products to Year 2000 compliance."[5]

This information is rather disturbing considering the potential effect this could have on industry, but what about the individual? Why is the information that is available only addressing the larger issues? Of course the larger issues are important. Yet, as with many other reports, this FAA report falls frighteningly short of addressing all the potential issues, especially to the average citizen. Questions about traveling plans on and around the Millennium should arise in our minds. The potential economic effects it can have on those who own stock in airline companies, computer companies, shipping companies, or any company providing services using even one computer to process date sensitive information could be exhaustive. Y2K has the potential to affect us all.

Social Security

Here is where this ambiguous little computer glitch starts to seem more concrete and hits us right between the eyes. Millions of Americans rely on Social Security for monthly support, medical assistance, and financial help in the event of a disabling injury or disease. Nearly every computer involved in processing and disbursing these moneys computes date sensitive information.

Before we go any further, though, you might be thinking to yourself, "This just can't be. How could the government have missed such an all-encompassing potential crisis?" How many times do you remember working with a large number of people either in the workplace, within a family, or at your local church where a myriad of things must get done to accomplish a given task? In the process, several things get overlooked. Sometimes they are small and relatively insignificant, but other times they are paramount to the success of the task. As a result of things not getting done or being done in error, the entire task is in jeopardy.

Now then, let's get back to the topic of Social Security. Under this we also want to include the topic of Medicare/Medicaid. Social Security accounts receivable and accounts payable, Medicare/Medicaid check disbursements and any other function of Social Security or Medicare is in jeopardy. Imagine not receiving your monthly Social Security check or having a bill sent to you for services rendered from your doctor when Medicare was supposed to foot the bill. As you know, if you are a Medicare recipient, medical bills can be astronomical.

Let's suppose for a moment that these events happen at the same time; you don't receive a check from Social Security but you do receive a bill from your doctor. So, you're left in a sticky situation, to say the least. Your first thought might be to call the Social Security office but when you dial all you get is a busy signal due to the hundreds or thousands who are calling in with similar issues. You may not even get a dial tone depending on how well the communication industry deals with Y2K.

Tired yet? Well, this scenario could be averted completely with the proper planning but you probably realize by now that full compliance of all computers is close to impossible. Again, we are not suggesting you read this book to decide "if" anything will happen, but to realize how damaging this problem will be "when" it happens.

Strange Laws

This section is going to shock you (as if every page up to this point hasn't been alarming). Probably, most susceptible to finding extreme issue with the following information are the dooms-dayers, end times fanatics, and every person who belongs to any "X Files" fan club.

There are some extremely strange laws that have been enacted throughout this century that, when mentioned, will at least cause you to raise an eyebrow and, in extreme cases, will cause some to "head for the hills." We wouldn't recommend the latter of these two options but we would suggest more than a coincidental nod. These laws are supposed to be for the betterment of the people of these United States in the event of extreme crisis.

One other point to consider before we give any examples of law is that Y2K could cause enough problems even as early as January of 1999 to prompt the government to declare a state of national emergency. This declaration would allow the government to activate their rights under the following laws, which are actually Executive Orders from current and pre-Clinton administrations. Edward Bell summarizes most of the Orders that directly affect the private citizen.

Order # -   **Description**

10995 -   Seizure of all communications media in the United States.
10997 -   Seizure of all electrical power facilities, fuels and minerals, both public and private.
10998 -   Seizure of all food supplies and resources, public and private, and all farms and farm equipment.
10999 -   Seizure of all means of transportation, including personal cars, trucks, or any vehicles of any kind, along with total control over all highways, seaports and waterways.

11000 -	Conscription of U.S. citizens for work forces under federal supervision, including the splitting up of families, if deemed necessary.
11001 -	Seizure of all health, welfare, and education facilities, public and private.
11002 -	Empowers the Postmaster to register all men, women, and children in the U.S.
11003 -	Authorizes seizure of all airports and aircraft.
11004 -	Seizure of any and all housing to facilitate forced relocation of citizens from areas declared "unsafe." Also, to relocate of entire communities.
11005 -	Seizure of all railroads, inland waterways, and storage facilities, public and private.
11051 -	Provides the office of emergency planning complete authorization to put the above orders into effect in times of increased international tension, or economic or financial crisis.[6]

Basically, in the event of a national emergency, the government has the legal right under these laws to control virtually everything. Who do you think decides when we are in a national disaster? That's right, the government, and more specifically, the President decides on the state of the nation at any given time. So, in essence, the government can decide when the government can take control of all aspects of our lives to "reduce, to a small degree, the catastrophic effects this [Y2K] crisis will have on the unprepared masses."[7]

What does the current administration have to say about the power it has to take control of the nation? Well, it probably won't surprise you at this point to inform you of an Executive Order President Clinton signed in 1994 which reiterates the power given to the government in times of crisis. Order **12919** gives the president the right to "assume the power to control all transportation, regardless of ownership, all forms of energy, all farm equipment, all fertilizer, all food resources, all food resource facilities, all health resources, all metals and minerals, and all water resources."[8] In addition, Clinton signed Order **13010** in July 1996, which, in effect, gave him further jurisdiction over "telecommunications, electrical power systems, gas and oil storage and transportation, banking and finance systems, transportation capability, water supply systems, and emergency services (medical, police, and fire dept.)."[9] During a national crisis the power available to the one person who holds the office of United States President is staggering!

Other laws are on the books that might be cause for alarm. They include the Expedited Funds Availability Act of 1987, many laws resulting from the "War on Drugs," and the War Powers Act of 1917. These laws allow the government to do everything from limiting the amount of funds we can withdraw from our own accounts to keeping us from "trading with the enemy" which could include our own neighbors if they are considered "enemies of the state."[10]

In any event, the government is prepared to help you, the "unprepared" citizen, in the "unlikely" event of a national emergency. The only reason you are unprepared is because you do not have the right information. That is why we have written this book. As you continue reading, the chapters that follow will give you insights from our extensive research and suggestions for how you can prepare for the coming Millennium.

• Chapter 4 •

Y2K and the Economy

"I came here today because I wanted to stress the urgency of the challenge...All told, the world wide cost will run into the tens, perhaps the hundreds of billions of dollars, and that's the cost of fixing the problem, not the cost if something actually goes wrong."
President Bill Clinton, July 14, 1998[1]

"Without proper attention, the consequences of the Year 2000 problem will be costly and disruptive. Thousands of computers, running everything from telephone networks to financial markets, are threatened with failure. Even institutions that have fixed their own internal problem will feel the ripple effects from problems occurring externally."
The Merrill Lynch Forum[2]

At this point, it seems rather trivial to say that the Y2K issue may have a severe effect on our economy. Fair warning, though, this may be the point where you think to yourself, "this is information overload," or "there is no way this can possibly be this big of a deal," and you might begin to tune out the information you are reading. Yet, even though too much information might numb your senses to the effects of Y2K, we feel obligated to inform you of the possible damage that Y2K could have on our economy. Then, and only then, can you make informed, rational decisions for you and your family.

Our National Economy

A Stamford, Connecticut consulting firm polled 1,100 computer industry executives and a whopping 38% said they personally were considering pulling their assets from banks and other institutions before January 1, 2000.[3] Even as we type statistics like these, we even find it hard to swallow, but there is overwhelming evidence to suggest that those who are "in the know" are taking steps to lessen the impact of the Y2K inevitability. They are not just taking corporate steps to alleviate the damage to industry, they are systematically reorganizing their private finances to guard against economic recession scenarios. Why would they do that?

The Federal Reserve is trying to address the potential drain of cash by citizens from the nation's banks and financial institutions by increasing U.S. currency reserves in the coming year (1999). In fact, the Fed has already decided to increase currency inventories by at least a third, which amounts to 50 billion dollars. This is the first time the Fed has planned for a nationwide demand for extra cash.[4]

USA Today, in an article dated August 20, 1998, quoted banking scholar Martin Mayer as saying, "nobody knows how much is enough for Y2K-related nationwide demand because no one knows whether Y2K will be a glitch or a crisis."[5] The Fed could inject up to 150 billion dollars if demand rises beyond current expectation which is around $450 for each of the 70 million U.S. households.[6]

The economy is obviously inescapably tied to a myriad of different variables such as Y2K's effect on communications, transportation and power. Federal Communications Commission Chairman William Kennard in a recent testimony to the Senate stated, "[Y2K] has the potential of disrupting communications services worldwide."[7] The U.S. Government's General Accounting Office issued a report stating, "The public faces a high risk that critical services provided by the government and the private sector could be severely disrupted by the Year 2000 computer crisis. Financial transactions could be delayed, flights grounded, power lost, and national defense affected."[8] This report warns us that we face a "high risk" because of this "crisis."

Add this all up and what do you get? We don't have the answer. Clearly, though, the alarm is being sounded at all levels of the government.

Some are saying that this computer glitch "could cause a worldwide economic depression that lasts a decade."[9] When asked if Y2K was at a crisis level, 94% of information technology managers polled said yes. Forty-four percent of U.S companies have already experienced problems. These problems are going to get worse as time passes. The potential for this bug to affect our economy to the point of fostering an extended recession is real. The extent of the recession is up for debate but most agree that Y2K will, at the very least, effect the economy in the short term.

The Global Economy

There is one fact that quite possibly is the most frightening and downright depressing fact in this whole issue. After ingesting all of this information about our nation's lack of readiness for the Year 2000 Computer Problem, we find that we are in the lead in the race to solve Y2K. That's right! The United States is at the top of the readiness list, or it might be better to say that the United States is the least unprepared. No other nation is adequately addressing this crisis and some are even looking to the United States for help. - What an irony.

In March of 1998, Australia's Year 2000 efforts, thus far, resulted in an announcement that the Australian government would not meet the January 1, 2000 deadline, nor would Australia's largest businesses.[10] Other countries are lining up to suggest that they, too, may not be able to meet the deadline. Noted Y2K expert, Gary North, makes a sobering comment that, "it took [him] from early 1992 until late 1996 to comes to grips emotionally with the year 2000 problem . . . we are running out of time."[11]

The effects on the global economy, like our nation's economy, could be only a short-term problem or a catastrophic meltdown. We must consider the information that is available and prepare individually for the results of Y2K. In the chapters that follow we will attempt to point you in the right direction as to what options are available to you for protecting your savings and investments, your home, your family and your possessions. Please read carefully the ideas we present and use the resource list in the back to help you to begin actively pursuing the best avenues for the protection of the things and people you hold dear.

• Chapter 5 •

How will it affect me?

"...the Year 2000 problem is a very serious threat to the global economy. If the supply of information is disrupted, many economic activities will be impaired, if not entirely halted."
Dr. Edward Yardeni, Chief Economist
at Deutsche Morgan Grenfell[1]

"You try to draw money from an ATM and it refuses, even though you know you have money in your account. Your bank's computer thinks it is January 1, 1900 - and you weren't a customer then."
Edward Kelley Jr., Federal Reserve Board Governor, quoting from a report of the Computer Information Center of the UK[2]

Once the average individual is over the denial or shock that something of this magnitude could actually happen, the next question is: How will this directly effect me? The potential effects are numerous. Note that we say "potential." It is possible that you could lose your electricity, water, gas, and many other conveniences that you depend on directly. It is also possible that you could lose many forms of transportation, communication, and financing. It is also possible that you will experience relatively few problems directly. The reality is that everyone will be affected in some way.

Geographically the effects of the problem will vary, depending on the county, state, and nation in which you live. Yet, many of these effects could be universal.

Once again, we must point out that we do not have any evidence as to what will really happen at the turn of the millennium. We know that there will be problems, but we simply cannot know the magnitude. It is possible that the problems that occur could turn out to be nothing more than an inconvenience to you.

Electricity

The largest potential problem is the loss of electricity. If we lose electricity for any extended period of time the effects will be dramatic. We use electricity almost every minute of every day. We use it for light so we can work. It is used for heat to keep our families warm. We use it at work to operate our computers. Every cash register in every store uses it. The water in our homes is delivered through electric pumping stations. Every gas station uses it to pump gas. Not to mention the fact that all of our banks must have electricity to even open the doors.

It is clear that electricity is a vital utility. At this time, lawmakers have concluded that the power industry will not be 100% ready.[3] It would seem obvious that cooperative actions would have been taken by now, by the utilities, to share solutions and best practices to avert any power failures. But, this is not the case.

In a recent congressional hearing, Cathy Hotka, vice president of information technology at the National Retail Federation, said:

"Utilities are, so far, unwilling to share the results of their (year 2000) tests. One company is unwilling to rat on the other, and they seem to think they'll have legal trouble if they do...Our members don't know if they're going to have power or a (telephone) dial tone come Jan. 1, 2000."[4]

Just how is the electricity in jeopardy? To begin with your electric bill is based on the amount of electricity used over a given period of time. The computers that calculate your bill are all date dependent. If there is a problem with the computers your bill might be very small (great) or very large (not so good). And then there is the possibility that your electricity might get turned off because the computer thinks that you are 100 years overdue on your bill.[5]

Over and above the billing process for electricity, you must take into account the process by which electricity is produced and distributed - it is all automated. This automation is controlled and run through numerous microprocessors and computers, many of which are embedded into the system. These microprocessors and computers, if left untouched, could be a problem.[6]

Transportation

Many of us don't ever consider how valuable transportation is to our lives. Most things that we have or use were brought to us from another location. Without ships, planes, trains and trucks to deliver the goods we depend upon for our daily activities, our towns will come to a grinding halt.

The gas we use in our cars is brought over by ships. Most ships use computer aided engines for power. They also use satellite based Global Positioning Systems (GPS) to maneuver through shipping channels and to avoid weather problems.

Most of the goods we depend upon are delivered from other states or nations. Food supplies that are delivered to our stores are transported in ships, trains and trucks. Mainframe computers manage the trains and the truck routes. The computers not only regulate the flow of the trains but they give the locations of the cars.

Many of the goods businesses use are brought in daily by airplanes. For the most part, computers control airplanes. Navigation, power, and air traffic are all dependent upon mainframe computers. In a recent article, it was reported that the Federal Aviation Administration (FAA) claimed that 40 of its older IBM mainframe computers had been successfully tested and were year 2000 ready. When questioned about the FAA's tests, IBM refused to endorse them. "We're not in a position to pass judgment on their tests because IBM was not involved in their testing," said IBM spokesman Mark Nelson. "IBM's position is that (the 3083s computer) should be replaced because of age and scarcity of parts...They're not year 2000 compliant."[7]

It is critical that these transportation links be compliant by the year 2000 or many of the goods we need and use won't be delivered.

Communication

Alan Simpson, President of Communication Links, Inc. said, "The ability to communicate is the essential cement that holds together the building blocks of our modern society".[8] This quote was given in a testimony before the US House of Representatives Subcommittee on Communications and the Year 2000 problem, and very clearly states the importance of communication.

Communications are infused into every aspect of our lives. We communicate daily with friends and family over the telephone. Businesses rely on the ability to communicate to other businesses and services. Financial markets operate through communications with other markets. The ability to transfer information is critical in control signals for power stations, electrical companies, and gas and oil pipelines. Computers also transfer the information to manage critical services such as water and sewage.[9]

The entire Internet is driven by computers with the ability to pass information over a series of wires that are computer switched and routed to other locations. In June we had just one communications satellite spin out of control and millions were effected by its loss.

Furthermore, at a hearing of the U.S. Senate Special Committee on the Year 2000 Technology Problem, federal officials expressed concerns about international readiness, which could be a big problem for banks, brokerages and manufacturers that rely on foreign carriers. "It's fine if the US networks are ready, but so what? We're concerned about operations in Europe and Asia," said Peter A. Miller, Chief

Information Officer at J.P. Morgan and Co. in New York, after testifying at the hearing.[10]

Without the ability to communicate or pass data from one location to another the economy as we know it would be in trouble.

Finance

Last, but not least, we turn to the banking and financial institutions. Even attempting to adequately discuss the complete effects of the Millennium Bug on our financial institutions would require a book of its own. The global economy as we know it encompasses millions of networks and computers. It is through their communications that the world's wealth is transferred from nation to nation, business to business and person to person. Markets worldwide rely on the computer to buy and sell. Banks conduct all of their business through computers. The government prints Social Security checks by computer. Your credit card payments are transferred electronically from one bank to another. If even a small percentage of these systems went down for a short period of time, the global economies could suffer.

International economist Don Smith at HSBC Midland was quoted as saying, "No one really has a clue just how big the problem will be. We have never experienced anything like it before. There's a huge interdependency between systems which makes predicting the results of computer failure an impossible task, really."[11]

How serious is the Year 2000 threat to the banking community? The following is a letter from the Board of Governors of the Federal Reserve to its Bank Officers. We will let you read and analyze the letter. Note the last sentence in the second paragraph.

"TO THE OFFICER IN CHARGE OF SUPERVISION AND APPROPRIATE SUPERVISORY AND EXAMINATION STAFF AT EACH FEDERAL RESERVE BANK AND TO EACH DOMESTIC AND FOREIGN BANKING ORGANIZATION SUPERVISED BY THE FEDERAL RESERVE.

SUBECT: The Federal Reserve's Intensified Year 2000 Compliance Efforts

Assuring that computer systems and applications are Year 2000 compliant presents a complex managerial and technological challenge for all enterprises, both public and private. For entities such as financial institutions that rely heavily on computers to provide financial services to customers, achieving Year 2000 compliance in mission critical systems is essential not only for maintaining the quality and continuity of the services, *but also for assuring the very survival of the entity itself.*

While bank supervisors can provide guidance, encouragement, and strong formal and informal supervisory incentives to the banking industry to address this challenge, the supervisors cannot be responsible for ensuring or guaranteeing the Year 2000 readiness and viability of each system used by the banking institutions they supervise. Rather, the boards of directors and senior management of banks and other financial institutions must shoulder the responsibility for ensuring that the institutions they manage are able to provide high quality and continuous services beginning on the first business day in January of the Year 2000 and beyond. This critical obligation must be among the very highest priorities for bank management and boards of directors."[12] (emphasis added)

Has the finger pointing already begun? If the Year 2000 problem was not going to have a large impact why would the FED use the terms, "for assuring the very survival of the entity itself... very highest priorities." It is clear that the FED is also alarmed.

Dr. Gary North stated, "Something in the range of 75% to 80% of this decision-relevant information is stored on mainframe computers". He went on to say, "The smooth operation of the free market is totally dependent on a continuing flow of accurate information."[13] Our entire economic system is run in some way by computers.

In a July 1998 article in Computerworld Magazine an interesting point was made. Of the 4,260 corporations that file reports with the SEC, only four firms reported that they've progressed with complete systems testing.[14]

It is critical that you understand the scope of this problem. It is possible that you will not be able to write checks for a period of time. It is possible that your ATM will not work. In the confusion, it is possible that records receipts and transcripts could be lost. The results of any one of these systems failing to be ready for 2000 could be damaging. The question to be asked is, "How many of these systems will be Y2K compliant in time?" We will soon find out. The one comforting thought is that if any industry has the money and resources to achieve compliance, it is the financial industry. But do they have the time?

• Chapter 6 •

What Can I Do?

"The time for awareness is absolutely over, It's time for some action."
U.S. Representative Constance Morella (R.Md.)[1]

"Strategic planning for the year 2000 computer bug is crucial to your survival and comfort in the months and years ahead. You are going to have to sharpen your own self-reliance skills rather than relying on the government, or major corporations, if you are to be prepared for the coming "Zap" from the Millennium Bug."
Craig Smith[2]

Prior to moving into action there are two points you must consider. The first and most important is a comprehension of the problem. Without a thorough understanding of the problem it will be impossible for you to prepare for all areas critical to your planning. As we have said before, following the completion of this book we highly encourage you to continue studying the problem from the wealth of sources in print and on the Internet. By fully understanding the depth of the problem you should be able to put together a good risk analysis on the potential impacts to your city and family.

Therefore, after understanding the problem and prior to taking action it is critical that you do a risk analysis. You should start by identifying risks to your city and family. Do you live in a big or small city? What are some problems that could arise in my city? Am I serviced by a large or small telephone company? Is my bank ready or planning to be ready for the Year 2000? You should take a look at the likelihood of one or all of the topics in the preceding chapter occurring, then evaluate and assess how the potential impact of those areas affect you.

After understanding the risks, the next step is to eliminate some of the risks in advance. The best way to handle risks is to stop the problem before it ever occurs. If you knew for sure that you would be without electricity for two weeks, would you buy a generator, would you stock up on candles and batteries?

The last step is to plan to minimize the impacts of the risks that do occur. Most of us will not be able to take all of the steps to eliminate all of the potential problems, but we can prepare to react to some of the problems that do arise. Being able to identify risks and plan a course of action will be paramount in reducing the impact of the Y2K problem.[3]

Following a complete understanding of the problem and after putting together a plan to eliminate risks, you must take action. In the following paragraphs we will bring up several proactive plans that need to be considered in your actions. We will not go into great depth in covering all of the concepts but we hope to give you enough to get started. The following is a list of possible actions that, if taken, could benefit you in the Year 2000 Problem.

(We must point out that we are not professional financial advisors nor are we experts in these fields. We highly encourage you to seek a professional advisor to answer any questions. The following is simply a compilation of ideas that could help to protect you and your assets. There is no perfect solution to one of the most complex problems you could ever face. We encourage you to research each of these ideas and make a decision that is right for you based on the information you have gathered and your own convictions.)

Next to your personal safety, which we will cover later, the most important issue is your money. Protecting your financial assets will be critical as we move into the next century.

Diversification and Documentation

The two most important points in protecting your assets are Diversification and Documentation. It will be critical that you diversify your investments into investments that are safe, easily liquidated and or tradable. Investments such as properties, land, gold, silver, and food sources could be a good start to diversifying because they offer intrinsic value.[4]

In a recent article, Don't Wait Until the Exits are Clogged, Tony Keyes stated, "Electronic assets are at greatest risk."[5] Electronic assets could be of no value if they can not be obtained. You want to make sure that you can access your assets at all times.

Other solid investments during market uncertainty could be investing in industries that are involved in fixing the Year 2000 problem. In fact there are now several indexes listing Y2K companies.

Y2K expert Ed Yourdon said, "Diversification has become a religion for me this year...I suggest that you don't put all of your eggs in one basket. Flexibility and liquidity are critical in the days ahead both financially and psychologically."[6]

Documentation will probably be the easiest and most effective way of protecting all of your assets. In today's electronic age, most of our records are kept electronically. By documenting all of your investments and assets you are providing yourself with a certain amount of insurance going into the Year 2000. Start by obtaining multiple proofs of identification including the following: your Social Security card, birth certificate, drivers license, voter registration card and passport. The burden of proof will always be on you. The following is a short list of records that you should copy and have in your possession (you will probably think of others - this is just to get you thinking):

- Tax Returns
- Bank Accounts and Statements
- Insurance Forms
- 401K and Stock Accounts
- Credit Card Statements
- Electricity Bills and Phone Statements
- Mortgage
- Auto Loans
- Misc. Loans
- Business Contracts
- Wills and Deeds
- Health and prescription plans
- Safe deposit contracts
- Veterans benefits statements
- Social Security accounts
- Medicare accounts

Possible Steps

At your bank, you should begin by asking questions. Most of the proactive banks already have in place information lines and or flyers documenting their position and progress toward Y2K. If a bank fails to acknowledge Y2K or fails to put in writing their Year 2000 readiness, you might consider switching banks. It is important that they state that they are "100% Y2K Compliant". Many of the financial institutions are very close to being 100% Y2K Compliant. Your financial institution should have this in writing by the Fall of 1999.

We must point out that if the Year 2000 problem is big enough to cause one bank to fail, then it will probably cause many to fail. The typical savior in the case of a bank failure is the FDIC. The only problem with the FDIC is that you would have to fill out an application to get your money back. That application would be placed in line with thousands of others. It could take months, if not years, to get your money back. This scenario does not even take into account the potential problems the FDIC could have with Y2K and its own computers.[7] If several banks fail and the FDIC can not come to their rescue, then it is possible that we could be in for some major problems.

In England, the problems are the same. In the foreword to a Year 2000 publication, Eddie George, the Governor of the Bank of England, said, "The financial system - especially in a centre as large and diverse as London - is highly interdependent and the failure of one quite small part can easily have substantial knock-on effects. And the failure of parts of the infrastructure could be catastrophic."[8]

There are those individuals who are concerned about not having access to cash during the first several weeks of 2000. This fear is a possibility if there is no electricity and if the banks are working the bugs out of their system. Remember, though, that banks have been around long before computers and even electricity. Many banks can still function by doing all of the transactions manually. You might have to be patient in line but you should still have access to your money. However, if something happened that put the major banks in trouble then the smaller ones could follow and you might not get access to your money for a while. If you are concerned about this happening to your bank, you might consider taking out enough money to last you for a set period of time.

There are others who are concerned about the value of the dollar. Should something happen that adversely effects our banking and governmental system, the value of the dollar would be hurt as well. If there becomes a lack of confidence in the dollar, the ability to purchase with it would be hindered. Paper money only has value as long as the general public has faith in the government. If certain departments within the government were to fail, then that faith could erode. This occurrence is where gold and silver come in. Many experts feel that if, in the worse case scenario, the dollar fails then gold and silver would be a good investment.[9] Both have a worldwide value and are easily liquidated.

Barter is the last form of currency that arises out of a crisis. People trade possessions with others for the goods and services they need. Barter is the oldest means of exchanging goods and the most widely used outside of paper money. Stocking up on such items as canned goods, coffee, tea, toilet paper and sugar could be useful if barter becomes the means of currency.[10]

Debt is not good in any year, but particularly in 1999. If you have credit cards we encourage you to get out of debt which would alleviate any concerns about mistakes in your billing or problems with your inability to pay during a slow economy. Regardless of the problem ahead, getting out of debt is just good business.

In the case of your mortgage, always look ahead. If you can, we encourage you to pre-pay several months in advance, eliminating any concerns about problems in the payment process during the first couple months of 2000. As always make sure you get receipts and keep copies of the canceled checks. Also, check with your mortgage company to make sure that your property taxes and homeowners insurance are paid. In some cases there might be a small fee for pre-payment, always ask if they will waive that fee. Most likely if your bank fails and you were unable to write a check to cover your mortgage you won't be evicted. As always though, it is better to be safe than sorry.

Regarding investments, we again would recommend that you have documentation on all of your accounts and stocks. We also would encourage you to get a letter from your broker stating that they have correctly addressed Y2K. If you are uncomfortable leaving your stocks in the account you could always ask for the stock certificates. The last thing you want to have happen is for your entire portfolio to be wiped out with the changing of date. For the millions of you who have mutual funds you might consider changing your portfolio to a more conservative position. If you are in the market for the long run then a down time in the market should not bother you, but be prepared.

It is also critical that you have researched the companies in which you are currently investing. Let's say you have 10,000 shares of company XYZ. Company XYZ is a small computer company specializing in Y2K solutions. XYZ has been working on several large corporate computer systems. Following our entry into the new millennium it is discovered that they had missed several thousand lines of text and the computer systems of these corporations freeze up. These major corporations now have to shut down for several months while they repair their billing and inventory systems. Thousands are temporarily out of work, the stock prices of the corporations fall and the company that worked on the problem is sued. The stock you now hold is worthless because the company had to pay millions in damages and declared bankruptcy. Whether you have stock in the major corporation or in the small computer company, you as the stock holder could be adversely affected.

Financial Markets

"Wall Street is seriously ignoring Y2K," said Ed Yourdon author of Time Bomb 2000. Yourdon went on to say, "Wall Street is the engine driving our global economy - yet Y2K denial is rampant." Whether Wall Street is ignoring the issue or whether they see it as a non-issue is unclear. In truth, if Y2K turns out to have a negative impact on public companies, then Wall Street will definitely feel it.

Investors have mixed emotions about Y2K. While many believe that a market slide at the end of 1999 would be devastating, others will see it as an opportunity. In every down market there are those investments that will excel. In this particular market an area of interest will be the Y2K solution companies. Merrill Lynch expects the final cost of the Year 2000 Bug to reach 1 trillion dollars.[11] Those companies who position themselves correctly could benefit greatly from Y2K. As a vendor in the Year 2000 industry, this will be a great time. Companies concerned with their survival will become desperate and make no complaints about paying large sums for a solution. J.P. Morgan Securities Inc. reported, "Beyond 2000, a new industry will emerge to sell fixes for the Year 2000 "temporary fixes" that were put in place in haste to make the deadline."[12] It is clear that the Year 2000 industry will have several years of good business.

Financially, there is some hope. J.P. Morgan Securities Inc. stated, "Despite some industry observers' projections that many companies will not make the necessary changes in time, we believe most will come up with a solution in time to remain operational after the start of 2000."[13] Its good to be optimistic but unfortunately there are few facts to back up this opinion.

Responsible Individuals

We feel businesses, and the individuals that run those businesses, must be both proactive and honest about their progress towards Year 2000 compliance. "What?" you say, "Proactive and Honest!" YES. It is critical not only for the customers, investors and employees, but also for the business itself to be honest about its progress. The financial future of companies could be in jeopardy if they fail to achieve compliance and specifically if they fail to be up front about it. The river of litigation that could be brought on a company who fails to meet its deadlines and then lies about it would be enormous. Alan Simpson, before the House of

Representitives said, "It is essential that major banks, and corporations, inform and prepare their customers, investors, and suppliers for the possible impact of Y2K, and their progress towards a safe, and comfortable transition." [14]

It is critical that companies' management becomes proactive and aggressive at first solving the problem and second informing others about it. If you are reading this book and are in positions of influence in your company we highly encourage you to ask questions and create awareness. It will be people like you taking a stand and creating urgency who will have the biggest impact in solving the problem. Currently the biggest problem is lack of awareness.

Finally, it is critical that you act now. You are currently ahead of the game by reading this book. However, it will be worth nothing to you if you do not act. Y2KNET founder, Craig Smith said, "time is still on your side if you start taking action now. Next year it won't be!" [15]

• Chapter 7 •

Practical Safety Tips

With the worst case scenario being fairly severe, we felt it in the best interest of the reader to devote a chapter to basic health and safety tips to consider if things get bad. Please note that many of these plans could be irrelevant if the utilities in your area are not effected and the transportation links are uninterrupted. But as the old saying goes, "it is better to be safe than sorry."

Food and Water

The FEMA web site located at www.fema.gov has a wealth of information on emergency preparedness. The following paragraphs on emergency food and water supplies were taken from the Federal Emergency Management Agency (FEMA).

Water should be the top item on any Y2K preparation list. The human body can function for over a month without food but only three days without water. It is critical that you plan to have a supply of water, which will last your family. An active person needs about two quarts of water a day. In hot environments, this number doubles. Children, nursing mothers, and the ill will need more. You will need additional water for preparing your food and for personal hygiene. One gallon of water per day per person would be sufficient.

It is important that you never ration water. Drink what you need and then look for more water. You can minimize the amount of water your body needs by reducing activity and staying cool.

You will be able to store water in thoroughly washed plastic, glass, fiberglass or enamel-lined metal containers. Never use a container that has held toxic substances. Many of these items can be purchased from local suppliers.

It is important that prior to storing your water that you treat it with a preservative such as chlorine bleach to prevent the growth of microorganisms. Use liquid bleach that contains 5.25 percent sodium hypochlorite and no soap. Add four drops of bleach per quart of water (or two scant teaspoons per 10 gallons), and stir. Seal your water containers tightly, label them and store them in a cool, dark place.

If disaster comes upon you suddenly, there are many supplies of water in your house. You can use water in your hot water tank, in your plumbing and in your ice cubes.

To use water in your hot water tank, be sure the electricity or gas is off, and open the drain at the bottom of the tank. Start the water flowing by turning off the water intake valve on the tank and turning on a hot water faucet. Do not turn on the gas or electricity when the tank is empty.

To use water in your pipes, let air into the plumbing by turning on the highest faucet in your house and draining the water from the lowest one.

Waterbeds are another source of usable water as long as toxic chemicals were not added when the bed was installed. If you wish to use your waterbed as a source of emergency water, drain it yearly and refill it with fresh water containing two ounces of bleach per 120 gallons.

Other sources of water outside your home would include, rainwater, streams and rivers and other moving bodies of water. Ponds, lakes, and natural springs round out the list. Each of these sources needs to be purified before being consumed. Avoid water that has an odor or has floating material on or in it.

In any case, where you are unsure of the integrity of the water source you should purify it before drinking, cooking or using it for hygiene. There are many ways to purify water. None are perfect. Often the best solution is a combination of methods. Before purifying, let any suspended particles settle to the bottom, or strain them through layers of a paper towel.

Boiling is one of the safest methods of purifying water. Bring water to a rolling boil for 10 minutes (add 5 minutes for every 1000 feet above sea level), keeping in mind that some water will evaporate. Let the water cool before drinking. Another method of purifying water is chlorinating, which uses liquid chlorine bleach to kill microorganisms. Add two drops of bleach per quart of water (four drops if the water is cloudy), stir and let stand for 30 minutes. If the water does not taste and smell of chlorine at that point, add another dose and let stand another 15 minutes. You can also use chlorine or iodine purification tablets to treat your water. One tablet is usually enough for one quart of water. They are inexpensive and available at most sporting goods stores. Remember the best solution is often a combination of these methods. We recommend that you check with your local water company to see what would be best for the water in your area.

These measures will kill microbes but will not remove other contaminants such as heavy metals, salts, most other chemicals and radioactive fallout. Running the water through filters designed specifically for this purpose is recommended.

Distillation is a more intensive purification process but will help to remove the microbes, heavy metals, salts, most chemicals, and radioactive dust and dirt. Distillation involves boiling water and then collecting the vapor that condenses on the lid back to water. The water that drips from the lid is distilled.[1]

Good personal hygiene needs to be taken into consideration during a time of crisis. Make sure you have enough water to bathe and for flushing the toilet. Filling up the tub with water for use in flushing is a good idea.

It is critical that water be considered first when planning for Y2K survival.

Food will most likely be second on the list for most people in the planning stages. Unlike water, food can be rationed safely -- except for children and pregnant women. There is no need to go out and buy special food. You can use the canned foods, dry mixes and other staples in your pantry shelves.

Proper storage will be critical for short term and long term planning. The following is a list of storage tips:

1. Keep food in the driest and coolest spot in the house - a dark area if possible
2. Keep food covered at all times.
3. Open food boxes or cans carefully so that you can close them tightly after each use.
4. Wrap cookies and crackers in plastic bags, and keep them in tight containers.

5. Empty opened packages of sugar, dried fruits and nuts into screw-top jars or airtight cans to protect them from pests.
6. Inspect all food containers for signs of spoilage before use.

When stockpiling food for an emergency always keep in mind your family's unique tastes. Try to include foods that they will enjoy and that are also high in calories and nutrition. Foods that require no refrigeration, preparation or cooking are best. Individuals with special diets and allergies may need special attention in planning the proper foods.

It is also critical that you rotate your food supplies. Use the foods before they go bad, and replace them with fresh supplies, dated with a marker. Always inspect your food for damaged items or expired dates.

For long-term food supplies the best approach is to store large amounts of staples along with a variety of canned and dried foods. Bulk quantities of wheat, corn, beans and salt are inexpensive and have nearly unlimited shelf life. For long-term supplies it is recommended that you stock the following amounts per person, per month:

- Wheat - 20 pounds
- Powdered Milk in Nitrogen-packed cans (for babies and infants) - 20 pounds
- Corn - 20 pounds
- Iodized Salt - 1 pound
- Soybeans - 10 pounds
- Vitamin C - 15 grams

Store wheat, corn and beans in sealed cans or plastic buckets. And leave salt and powdered milk in their original packages. We recommend that you add additional vitamins and minerals to this group.

If these staples comprise your entire menu, you must eat all of them together to stay healthy. To avoid serious digestive problems, you'll need to grind the corn and wheat into flour and cook them, as well as boil the beans, before eating.

The above staples offer a limited menu, but you can supplement them with commercially packed air-dried or freeze-dried foods and supermarket goods. Rice, popcorn and varieties of beans are nutritious and long lasting. Remember, though, the more supplements you include, the more expensive your stockpile will be.[2]

Finally, if you have enough space in your backyard you can begin by growing a small garden. Gardens are a great source of fresh fruits and vegetables. Besides providing food for your family, they could be fun family projects.

Loss of Electricity

The loss of electricity is a big concern to most of us. The loss of electricity for a long period of time would alter our everyday activities dramatically. Preparing for the possibility of not having electricity requires some planning and thought. Two of the areas that need to be considered are Heat and Light.

Heat for your home could be shut off without electricity. Take steps to be prepared. Extra blankets and a good supply of wood for your fireplaces would work well. Other solutions include small generators to power space heaters. Kerosene heaters would also be sufficient to provide warmth. (NOTE - Please use space heaters and kerosene heaters wisely, for they are a severe fire hazard. Keep heaters three feet from all objects). It would be advisable to check with your local Fire Department in regard to emergency heaters. During the winter months, always try to layer your clothes and if necessary have your children sleep together to share heat.

Light is powered by electricity and is essential to see and to cook. Plan to have alternative lighting sources for a period of time, such as flashlights with plenty of extra batteries. Also, be prepared with a supply of candles and lanterns. Some candles have been designed to burn for up to 50 hours and are relatively inexpensive. (NOTE - Please, be careful to keep children and combustible items away from open flames.) Small generators would work well to provide power for a small quantity of lights. Try to restrict your major activities to the daytime hours. You might have to revert back to, "early to bed, early to rise." If your stove is electric, plan alternate methods of cooking. Small camping stoves are an excellent alternative, but remember to stock propane for them.

Other Concerns

Transportation could also be adversely affected by Y2K. With the majority of gas stations controlled by computer, the availability of fuel could be a problem. We do not recommend storing fuel. However, we recommend that you have a full tank on December 31, and try to limit the amount of driving you do during the first few days of 2000. Alternate sources of transportation such as bicycles and motor bikes could be useful during this time. We do not encourage long distance travel by any means in and around the beginning of the New Year. With the uncertainty of the effects of the Year 2000 Bug to airplanes, trains and boats, it would not be advisable to be far from home. If you do travel over the New Year, make alternate plans to stay a while. Also, beware of traffic signals and railroad crossings. Both are microprocessor controlled.

Communications could be inoperable for a while. This inability potentially includes phones, faxes, the Internet, cell phones, television and pagers. The best way to combat this problem is to have an alternate plan. Short wave radios and or CB Radios could be valuable in communicating to loved-ones and or, in the case of emergency, getting help. Receiving information also becomes critical in the time of crisis. Having a radio with plenty of batteries is essential. Finally, develop an emergency communication plan for the family. During a crisis, develop a plan where a third party or pre-set phone number could be called and all members can check-in.

General Supplies needed for Y2K survival could include: flashlight, portable radio, first aid kit, non-electric can opener, essential prescription medications, blankets, sleeping bags, fire extinguisher, stove, utensils, tent, camping tools, money, matches and a plan.

An excellent source of additional information on Y2K preparation is The Cassandra Project by Paloma O'Riley. You can find The Cassandra Project at http://www.millennia-bcs.com/prep.htm on the Internet.

Begin now to plan the appropriate actions for you and your family. Do not let January 1, 2000 surprise you. If you plan for an emergency and nothing happens, GREAT! Life goes on and so do you. (You shouldn't have to go to the store for a while.) But if something does happen, YOU WILL BE PREPARED.

(See Appendix B for a checklist to help you get started)

• Chapter 8 •

The Good News

This book is not a "feel good" reading opportunity. It speaks of crisis, danger, and potential devastation to our economy, our finances and our families. There is nothing we like less than having to share these things with you. However, we also have an opportunity to tell you about a light at the end of the tunnel.

Most of us experience feelings of anxiety and hopelessness when we read the pages of this book. We see the problem as too big for us to fathom. We look at the process we will have to go through to protect our family and possessions and know that even good planning may not guarantee freedom from the effects of Y2K.

In this country, one of the most cherished rights we possess is the pursuit of happiness. On the surface, this is an enviable right, but unfortunately many are slaves to the fact that circumstances in our lives determine our happiness at any given time. In other words, our happiness is cemented to the circumstances of our lives. If you buy a new car, you are happy; if you get a flat tire, you are not happy. If you get a good grade on a test, you are happy; if you fail, you are not happy. If you are rich, you are happy; if you are poor, you are not happy. If Y2K turns out to be nothing, then you are happy; if it plays havoc in all areas of your life, you are not happy. Right? Though, this should be true for all such examples this is not always the case.

When talking about happiness, we can continue using these types of examples to categorize ourselves as happy or unhappy according to our own personal circumstances, or we can look at another aspect of how we experience happiness. There is another word, that I want to put into the mix, and it is the word "joy." That's right, "joy." Joy is often used interchangeably with the word "happiness" but they are completely different. Having joy is NOT tied to your circumstances. In fact, you can have joy even when the circumstances are not good in your life.

If you find the secret of joy you can get a flat tire and still have joy. You can fail a test and still have joy. You can be poor and still have joy. Y2K can have a negative effect on you, your family and possessions, and you can still have joy. Happiness will be a very elusive emotion in the midst of economic and family crisis but joy will be available to everyone who knows what I'm about to tell you. Where can a person get joy? If you are asking this question, keep reading.

Think about it, it is easy to be happy when things are going well in your life. You don't have to try to be happy in that scenario, you just are. It would be incredible, though, if we could find a way to be "happy" when things aren't going well in our lives. If we could find a way to have peace, contentment, joy in the midst of this Y2K crisis, for example, we could bottle that formula and sell it to everyone. Well, we do have the formula for joy and it comes from an unlikely place and an unlikely person - and it's free!

A Guy Named Saul - - A True Story

Saul lived nearly two millenniums ago in a country the size of a postage stamp. He was a religious leader in his town. In fact, he was considered to be the religious leader of the religious leaders. He was a powerhouse in the community, kind of like a mayor or a CEO of a big company today. The guy was sharp as a tack, educated, strong-willed, and sure of himself. He and his counterparts had a good-ole-boy's club going and pretty much ran the town where they lived. This guy seemed to have it all - power, position, money and influence -- but he didn't have joy.

The government at the time was Rome and Saul was under the authority of Caesar, the ruler of the land. Saul and the other religious leaders were always on the lookout for groups of citizens who weren't sympathetic to their religion. When Saul found out that there was a religious group called "The Way" that looked at God from a completely different angle than he did, he got really angry. The Roman government found out about "The Way" and commissioned some men to go out and stop this radical group from gaining a foothold --

by any means necessary. The government gave Saul the legal right to arrest or kill anyone who said they were part of this group. I know that probably sounds extreme to you, but guys like Saul have gone out and done even worse things throughout history.

So Saul began to travel to different towns to root out the people who were part of this group. He found one of the leaders of "The Way" who was called Stephen. Stephen didn't bow down to the threats of Saul and the other leaders. However, this defiance gave Saul his first chance to make an example of one of these people, and he took advantage of it. He and his cohorts literally dragged Stephen out of the gates of the city, threw him down to the ground, and began to throw rocks at him. He cried out as they hit him, repeatedly bruising and breaking his body.

As this was going on, Saul actually stood there watching the men as Stephen was staggering helplessly. Stephen cried out, "Lord, Jesus, receive my spirit!" He fell to the ground moments after that, and cried out, "Lord, don't hold this sin against them!" and he breathed out for the last time. There lay the mangled body of Saul's first victim less than ten feet away -- this was only the beginning.

Saul saw Stephen's death as a gunshot marking the beginning of a sick and hateful race to end this 'movement' called "The Way". He went from house to house dragging men and women out of their homes. He put some in prison, killed others. There was one thing he couldn't understand, though. Many of these followers would not, under any level of torture, no matter how agonizing, recant what they professed to believe. The one name that every one of these followers proclaimed literally to their dying breath was - Jesus.

Saul wondered how these foolish people could believe so strongly in this Jesus; they would give up everything, even their very lives, for nothing more than a man. Something was different. He had seen other cults rise up against the establishment before, but none with followers so bold. He noticed that some, as they were beaten and lashed to death, seemed to actually be at peace in their final crisis. Saul was confused but kept to the task - stifle the rise of these followers of Jesus.

Saul went to the high priest not long after Stephen's death, his appetite whet with a desire for more prisoners, requesting a letter to continue his work against this group. He wanted to go to a town not far away called Damascus, and find more of these people who, curiously enough, seemed to be spreading their beliefs faster than even he could control.

He was walking with some people on a road headed for Damascus when something indescribably profound happened. A bright light flashed around him and he fell to the ground. Suddenly, he heard a voice say, "Saul, Saul, why do you persecute me?"

"Who are you, Lord?" Saul asked the voice.

"I am Jesus, the one you are persecuting. Now go into the city and you will be told what to do."

Saul rose to his feet but realized he had somehow been completely blinded! He was forced to ask the men who were with him to lead him by the hand into Damascus, the town where he was going to continue his attack against the group who followed this . . . "Jesus!"... He thought to himself, remembering the name of the voice that came out of heaven, only a moment before.

In Damascus, a man named Ananias, one of the followers of Jesus, met with Saul. Ananias had heard of Saul and was frightened at the thought of meeting him. When he found Saul he explained that Jesus had sent him there to help Saul "regain his sight and be filled with the Holy Spirit."

Not only was Saul's vision restored but he knew for the first time that the stories were true. He knew, he had actually met Jesus the man whose followers proclaimed him to be God Himself, who came to earth to save the world from their mistakes. He realized that he was living a life against the very God he thought he knew. He had attended church, he had done good things, he had prayed and read the Bible, but he suddenly realized that he had never experienced a personal relationship with God.

He now believed that Jesus was God, and that He died on a cross for the sins of the world. He believed that Jesus actually did rise from the dead three days later, as his followers bravely proclaimed time and time again until their dying breath.

He understood that all the things he had done to be religious had nothing to do with getting his address in heaven. His eyes were opened to the fact that Jesus really is the only way to get a relationship with God; not by doing good things, but by believing that Jesus paid for Saul's mistakes personally. At that moment Saul was born again. He became a follower of Jesus and went on to preach, teach and write many letters to the faithful followers.

Jesus talks in the Bible about being born again. He compares it to physical birth. For example, if you are born out of your mother's womb, what could you do to be unborn once you have been born? The answer is of course, nothing.

When we are born again in Jesus, it is a spiritual birth. With spiritual birth, we can never be spiritually unborn. We are brought into an eternal relationship with God and we will always be part of His family. Saul began that eternal relationship with God, through Jesus, that day in Damascus.

He learned that he actually had an eternal address in heaven with God and that he was breathing eternally. He also learned that God didn't just want him to look forward to heaven some day in the future, but he wanted to show Saul that he could actually be 'happy' here on earth regardless of his circumstances. God used a word for this ability to rise above the circumstances of the moment - JOY! That's right, the very thing we started this chapter with, this search for joy, comes from a relationship with God.

Think about Saul's life for a moment. He was a Christian killer, a murderer. Yet, though he killed and imprisoned people, Jesus forgave him and started an eternal relationship with Saul. Sounds crazy doesn't it? It's true! Not only did God forgive Saul through Jesus, he went on to show Saul the secret of joy!

At one point Saul was thrown in jail for his belief in Jesus. He was being treated just the same as he treated hundreds of other followers before he knew Jesus. Now understand, he is in prison, not sure if he will ever be freed. He writes a letter to some of his Christian family from prison and penned these words:

"....for I have learned to be content whatever the circumstances. I know what it is to be in need and I know what it is to have plenty. I have learned the secret of being content in any and every situation, whether well fed or hungry, whether living in plenty or in want. I can do everything through [Jesus] who gives me strength."[1]

Can you imagine being in prison and actually writing a letter that tells others about how much joy you have? Saul had learned the secret of being content regardless of what came his way - even prison! That secret was his personal relationship with Jesus Christ.

For most of his life Saul thought that he had to earn his place in heaven by doing good things. He thought that the whole thing was about religion; do this, don't do that, act this way, pray that way. He was trying to work his way to heaven. Religion is all about what man does in an effort to reach God. Yet, just as Saul found out, it's not about religion, or a philosophy of life, or a theory, but a real and intimate relationship with God Himself through Jesus. It **IS** all about a relationship; not what man can do to reach God, but what God has already done to reach man.

Like Saul, we are all born separated from God. "All have sinned: and fall short of God's ideal."[2] "But the trouble is that your sins have cut you off from God."[3] God wants to have a relationship with all of us, though, and has provided a way to get back to Him.

To find joy and purpose in life, you have to solve this problem of separation from God. We all must realize that, "The wages of sin is death, but the gift of God is eternal life through Jesus Christ."[4] The most incredible thing of all is that getting a relationship with God happens through Jesus Christ and it's a free gift! You don't deserve it. You can't do anything to earn it. You can't pay God for it - - IT'S FREE!

You might be thinking, "I'm doing too many things wrong to come to God and ask Him to forgive me." A lot of people think they have to get their act together before they can start a relationship with God. The opposite is true. In fact, "God demonstrates his own love for us in this: while we were still sinners, Christ died for us."[5] God shows us how much he loves each of us by starting a relationship even when we're right in the middle of making bad choices. He meets you right where you are, wherever that is!

So, if you can't earn your way to heaven, and God loves you enough to give you a way to meet him right where you are in life, the next step is to trust Jesus Christ by inviting Him to be the only one in charge of your life. "...If you confess with your mouth the Lord Jesus and believe in your heart that God has raised Him from the dead, you will be saved."[6] God wants to have a relationship with you and he has given you that opportunity if you will only accept what He has already done through Jesus for you.

Take the next step. If you recognize you are separated from God, and you are willing to turn toward Him; if you believe that Jesus died for you on a cross for all of your sins and overcame death; then invite Jesus to come and be the leader of your life.

Note: Just saying the words below does not mean anything unless you believe the things you're saying to God. Remember this is not about religion; it's not about getting all the words right. It's not a chant. It IS an opportunity for you to personally ask God to forgive you and bring you into His family.

What to say to God:

"I know my sin has separated me from you.
I believe You sent Jesus to die for me.
I ask You to forgive me.
I now turn my life over to You and receive Jesus as the leader of my heart and my life."

This new relationship with God is the secret of joy. Your slate has been wiped clean and you are a new creation! This is the beginning of an awesome new life in Jesus.

What next?

1. Get a Bible that you can understand.

2. Talk to God in prayer every day.

3. Tell someone what's happened to you.

4. Find a local church and start developing relationships with other Believers.

If you would like to talk to someone right now about your new relationship with Jesus or if you haven't made a decision yet and have some questions before you decide to give your life to Jesus, please call:

1-888-NEED-HIM

(24 HOURS A DAY, 7 DAYS A WEEK)

We hope and pray that you take to heart the words of this book. Time is truly of the essence. It is critical that you be informed and ready not only for Y2K but also for eternity. There are simple steps that you can take to prepare for both. We will continue to pray that God will bless you and this country through the good times and the bad.

Notes

Chapter One
1. www.comlinks.com/gov/test698.htm (Downloaded July, 1998)
2. http://www.comlinks.com/gov/aware1.htm (Downloaded July 1998)
3. http://www.mitre.org/research/y2k/docs/PROB.html (Downloaded July, 1998)
4. http://www.y2kinvestor.com/whatisy2k.htm (Downloaded July, 1998)
5. ibid.
6. http://www.yardeni.com/y2kbook.html (Downloaded July, 1998)
7. http://www.yrknet.com/news/98-2/global.htm (Downloaded July, 1998)
8. Ibid.

Chapter Two
1. http://comlinks.com/gov/csp0715.htm (Downloaded July, 1998)
2. http://comlinks.com/mag/forbes1.htm (Downloaded July, 1998)
3. http://comlinks.com/mag/cirep.htm (Downloaded July, 1998)
4. ibid.
5. http://y2kinvestor.com/whatisy2k.htm (Downloaded July, 1998)

Chapter Three
1. http://www.comlinks.com/mag/forbes1.htm (Downloaded July, 1998)
2. http://www.comlinks.com/gov/cp0715.htm (Downloaded July, 1998)
3. http://www.yardeni.com/y2kbook.html (Downloaded July, 1998)
4. ibid.
5. ibid.
6. http://www.y2knet.com/news/98-5/crisis.htm (Downloaded July, 1998)
7. Ibid.
8. Ibid.
9. Ibid.
10. Ibid.

Chapter Four
1. http://www.comlinks.com/gov/csp0715.htm (Downloaded July, 1998)
2. http://www.ml.com/woml/forum/millen.htm (Downloaded July, 1998)
3. http://www.y2knet.com/news/98-2/clogged.htm (Downloaded July, 1998)

4. Beth Belton, "A Stash of Cash for Y2K," USA Today, 20 August 1998, Money section, p. 1.
5. http://www.y2knet.com/news/98-2/clogged.htm (Downloaded July, 1998)
6. Ibid.
7. Larry Burkett, "Y2K: a 'real and serious' threat," Christian Financial Concepts, Issue 245, June 1998, p. 8
8. Ibid.
9. Ibid.
10. http://www.garynorth.com/y2k/search_.cfm (Downloaded July, 1998)
11. Ibid.
12. Ibid.

Chapter Five
1. http://www.y2kinvestor.com/intro.html (Downloaded July, 1998)
2. ibid.
3. www.computerworld.com/home/print.nsf/All/9805254F62 (Downloaded July 1998) Matt Hamblen, "Power plant panic," Computerworld Magazine, 25 May 1998
4. ibid.
5. http://www.Euy2k.com/intro.htm (Downloaded July, 1998)
6. ibid.
7. http://www.computerworld.com/home/print.nsf/all/9808035DF6 (Downloaded July, 1998) Matt Hamblen, "IBM, others question FAA's 2000 progress," Computerworld Magazine, 3 August, 1998
8. http://ww.comlinks.com/gov/test698.htm (Downloaded July, 1998)
9. http://www.comlinks.com/gov/test698.htm (Downloaded July, 1998)
10. http://www.computerworld.com/home/print.nsf/All/9807135A02 (Downloaded July, 1998) Matt Hamblen, "U.S. firms sweat foreign telco Y2K readiness," Computerworld Magazine, 13 July 1998
11. Neil Winton, http://www.timesofindia.com/today/02busi12.htm (Downloaded July, 1998)
12. http://www.bog.frb.fed.us/boarddocs/srletters/1998/sr9803.htm (Downloaded July, 1998)
13. Dr. Gary North, Remnant Review, p. 10.
14. http://www.computerworld.com/home/print.nsf/All/9805184B3A (Downloaded July, 1998)

Chapter Six
1. http://www.computerworld.com/home/print.nsf/All/9805254F62 (Downloaded July, 1998)
2. www.y2knet.com/news/98-5/crstw.htm (Downloaded July, 1998)

3. Edward Yourdon and Jennifer Yourdon, Time Bomb 2000: What the Year 2000 Crisis Means to You, (New Jersey: Prentice Hall, 1998)
4. http://www.y2knet.com/news/98-5/edtells.htm (Downloaded, July 1998)
5. http://www.y2knet.com/news/98-2/clogged.htm (Downloaded, July 1998)
6. http://www.y2knet.com/news/98-5/edtells.htm (Downloaded, July 1998)
7. Edward Yourdon and Jennifer Yourdon, Time Bomb 2000: What the Year 2000 Crisis Means to You, (New Jersey: Prentice Hall, 1998)
8. http://www.bankofengland.co.uk/pr98024.htm (Downloaded, July 1998)
9. http://www.y2knet.com/news/98-5/crstw.htm (Downloaded, July 1998)
10. ibid.
11. http://www.ml.com/woml/forum/millen2.htm (Downloaded July, 1998)
12. http://www.jpmorgan.com/MarketDataInd/Research/Year2000/Year2000_1.html (Downloaded July, 1998)
13. ibid.
14. http://www.comlinks.com/gov/test698.htm (Downloaded July, 1998)
15. http://www.y2knet.com/news/98-5/edtells.htm

Chapter Seven
1. http://www.fema.gov/library/emfdwtr.htm (Downloaded July, 1998)
2. ibid.

Chapter Eight
1. Philipians 4:11b-13 (New International Version - Unless otherwise noted, all scripture quoted is NIV)
2. Romans 3:23
3. Isaiah 59:2
4. Romans 6:23
5. Romans 5:8
6. Romans 10:9

Appendix A

Available Information

The following are books and web sites that are full of helpful information to keep you up to date on Y2K.

Books

- **Time Bomb 2000 - What the Year 2000 Computer Crisis Means to You!**
  Edward Yourdon and Jennifer Yourdon
- **Managing '00: Surviving the Year 2000 Computing Crisis**
  Peter De Jager and Richard Bergeon
- **The Millennium Bug - How to Survive the Coming Chaos**
  Michael S. Hyatt
- **The Year 2000 Computing Crisis - A Millennium Date Conversion Plan**
  Jerome T. Murray and Marilyn J. Murray
- **The Year 2000 Software Problem - Quantifying the Costs and Assessing the Consequences**
  Capers Jones
- **The Year 2000 Problem Solver - A Five Step Disaster Prevention Plan**
  Bryce Ragland

Internet Web Sites

www.garynorth.com
www.year2000.com
www.y2kstuff.com
www.y2k.com
www.y2klinks.com
www.safe2k.com

www.y2knet.com
www.y2kinvestor.com
www.millennia-bcs.com
www.y2ktimebomb.com
www.y2kwomen.com

Appendix B

Check List

- **Water**
  Storage Containers
  Liquid Bleach
  Iodine Tablets
- **Food**
  Storage Containers
  Canned Items
  Bulk Items
  Alternate Stove
  Propane
  Utensils
- **Heat**
  Blankets
  Firewood
  Sleeping Bags
  Generator
- **Light**
  Flashlight
  Batteries
  Lantern / Candles
- **Others**
  Portable Radio
  First Aid Kit
  Prescription Medication
  Can Opener – Non Electric
  Fire Extinguisher
  Money
  A Plan
  Information - The More, The Better!
- **Documentation – Records (see pg. 72)**
  Investments and Assets
  Legal Information
  Identification
  Bank Statements

Key Dates to Watch

The Y2K effect will be felt before January 1, 2000.

April 1, 1999 -   Start of Fiscal Year for Canada, Japan, New York, and other states.

September 9, 1999 -

Some programmers used 9/9/99 as a special value (ie.- infinity / shut down)

October 1, 1999 -   Start of Fiscal Year for the U.S. Government.

January 1, 2000 -   New Millennium.

NOTES

NOTES

NOTES

NOTES

NOTES

<u>NOTES</u>

Contact Information

To contact the authors for inquiries, speaking engagements, or for general information, call, write or e-mail:

Todd Phillips or Darren McMaster

800-647-1905

PO Box 780094
San Antonio, Texas 78278

info@safe2k.com

To order books call, write or e-mail:

SAFE 2000

800-647-1905

PO Box 780094
San Antonio, Texas 78278

info@safe2k.com

PLEASE ORDER A GOOD QUANTITY TO SHARE THE INFORMATION WITH OTHERS. Sorry, no C.O.D. or billing. Orders will be processed immediately upon receipt. The cost of one book is $14.95 + $3.50 shipping & handling.

If you would like us to ship one or more books to someone you know, please include $14.95 + $3.50 shipping and handling for each book. Also, the name, address and zip code of each to whom you are sending a book.